WATER, WATER EVERYWHERE, WHAT & WHY?
THIRD GRADE SCIENCE BOOKS SERIES

Speedy Publishing LLC
40 E. Main St. #1156
Newark, DE 19711
www.speedypublishing.com

Water is one of the most
important substances
on planet Earth.

Water is all over the Earth. Water covers around 70% of the Earth's surface.

97% of earth's water is in the oceans. The three largest oceans on Earth are the Pacific Ocean, the Atlantic Ocean and the Indian Ocean.

Only 2.5% of the Earth's water is freshwater. The source of almost all fresh water is precipitation from the atmosphere.

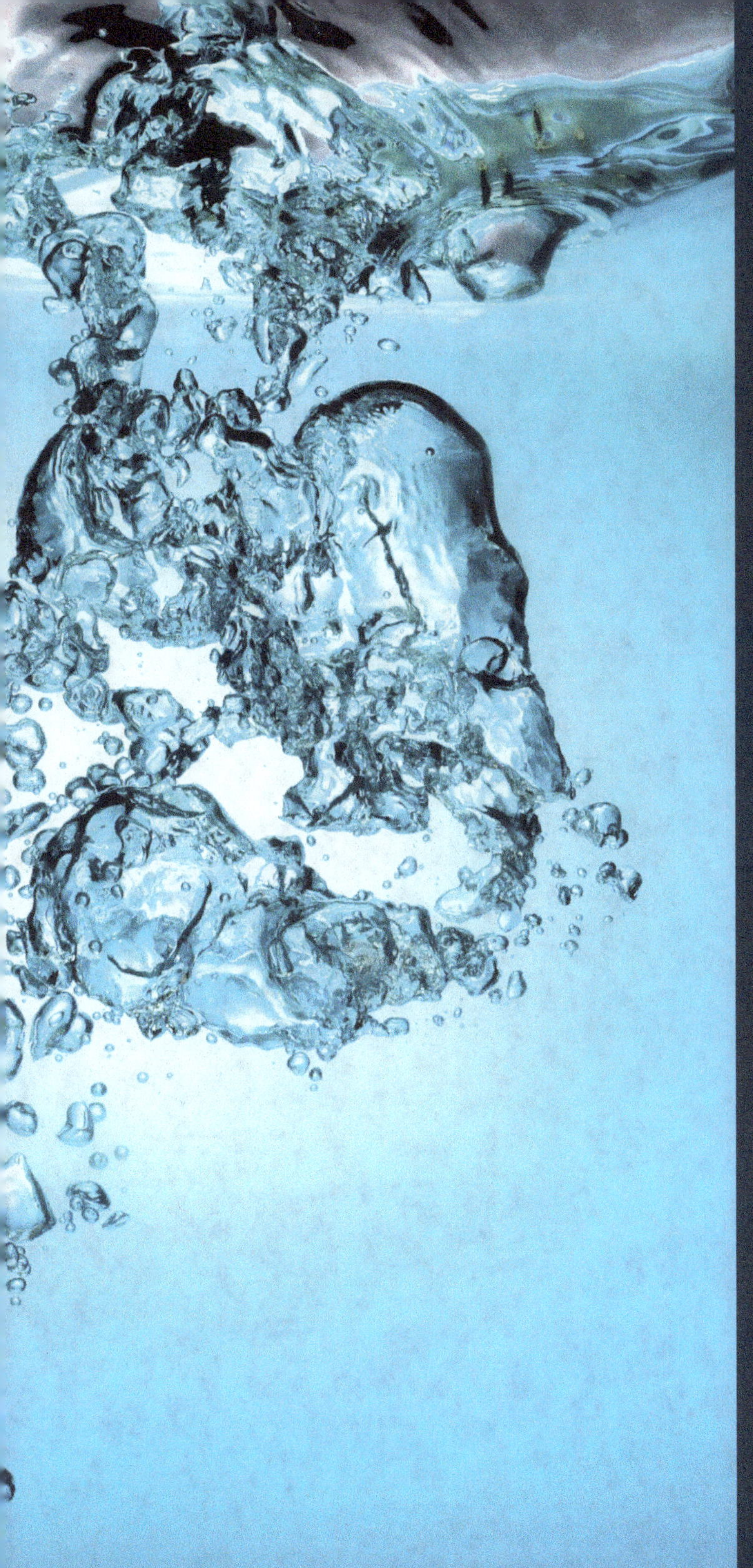

Pure water actually has no taste. What you taste when you drink tap water or bottled water is minerals and other substances that have dissolved in the water.

Ice is the solid form of water. When water gets below 0% C it will freeze and become ice.

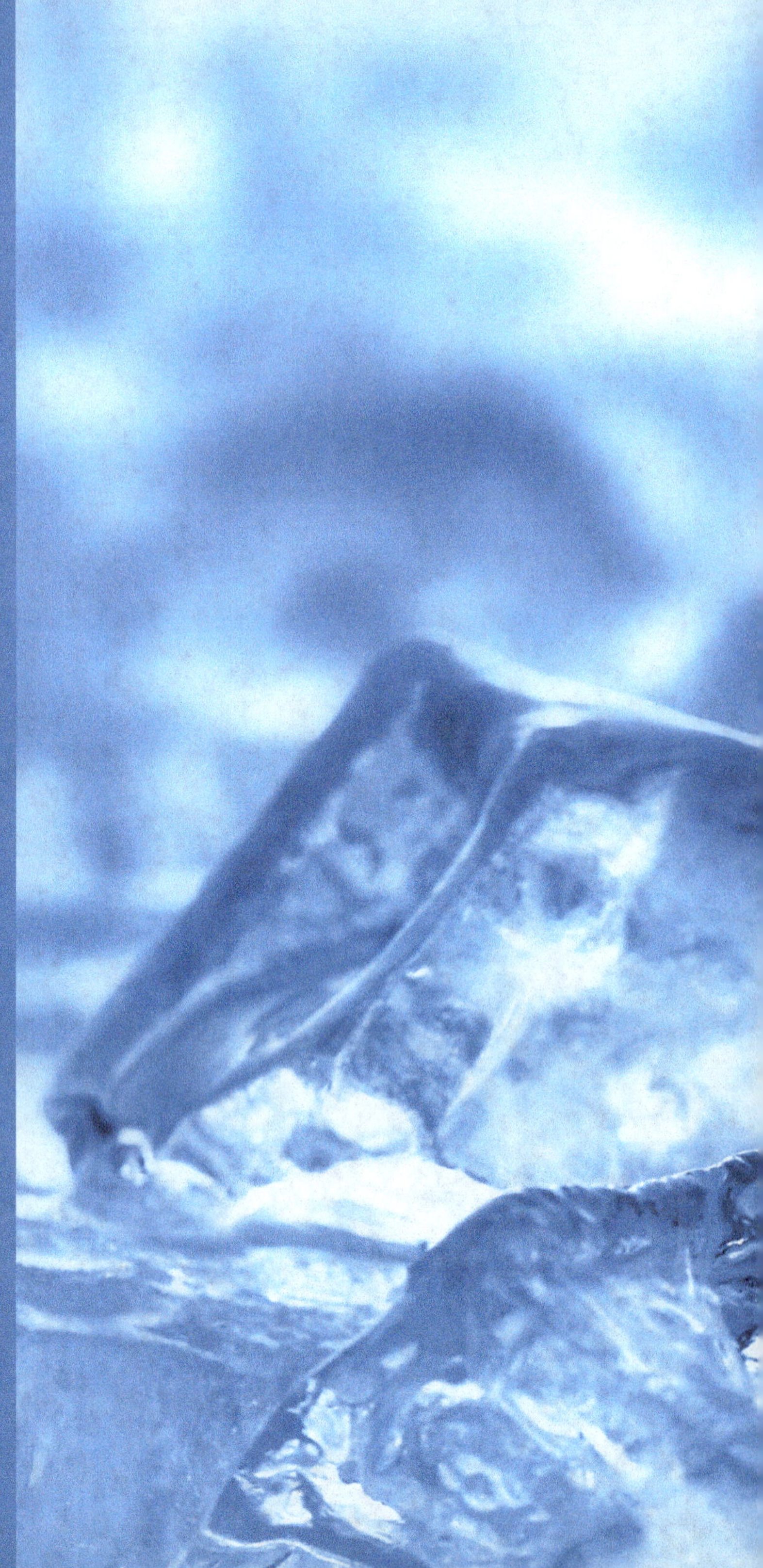

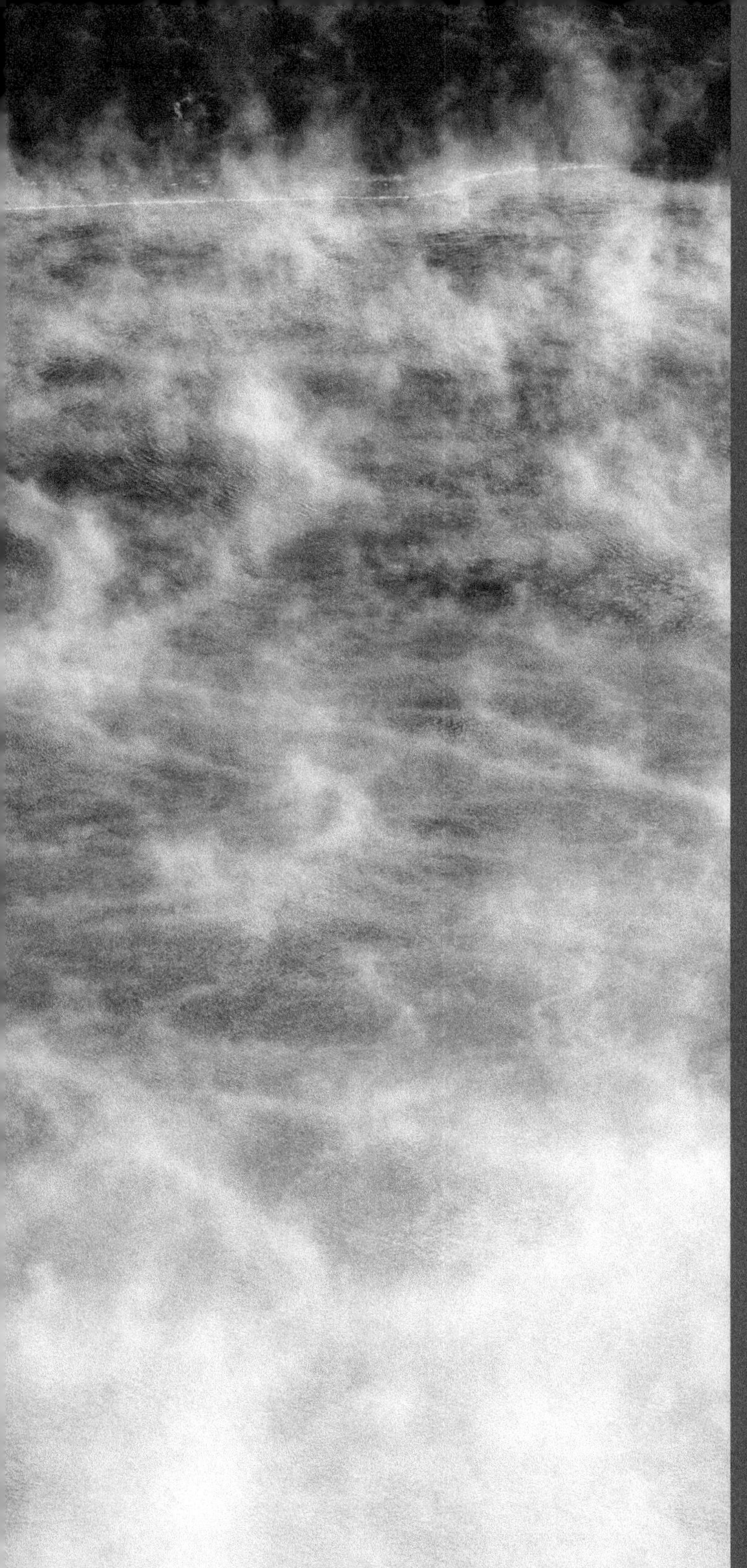

0.001% of the water is in the air as vapor, clouds, and precipitation. When the water gets above 100% C and starts boiling, water turns into its gas state called vapor.

2.4% of the Earth's water is frozen water in glaciers and the polar ice caps. Ice is less dense than water allowing giant icebergs to float on top of the ocean.